Q&A: Life's Mysteries Solved!

HOW DID DEATH VALLEY GET ITS NAME?

And Other FAQs About Geography

By Ryan Nagelhout

Gareth Stevens
PUBLISHING

Please visit our website, www.garethstevens.com. For a free color catalog of all our high-quality books, call toll free 1-800-542-2595 or fax 1-877-542-2596.

Library of Congress Cataloging-in-Publication Data

Names: Nagelhout, Ryan, author.
Title: How did Death Valley get its name? / Ryan Nagelhout.
Description: New York : Gareth Stevens Publishing, 2016. | Series: Q & A:
  life's mysteries solved! | Includes index.
Identifiers: LCCN 2016003831 | ISBN 9781482447330 (pbk.) | ISBN 9781482447354 (library bound) | ISBN
9781482447347 (6 pack)
Subjects: LCSH: Curiosities and wonders–Juvenile literature.
Classification: LCC AG243 .N26 2016 | DDC 031.02–dc23
LC record available at http://lccn.loc.gov/2016003831

Published in 2017 by
Gareth Stevens Publishing
111 East 14th Street, Suite 349
New York, NY 10003

Copyright © 2017 Gareth Stevens Publishing

Designer: Andrea Davison-Bartolotta
Editor: Kristen Nelson

Photo credits: Cover, p. 1 (desert) Vezzani Photography/Shutterstock.com; cover, p. 1 (vulture) sharpner/iStock/
Thinkstock; pp. 4, 6, 9, 12, 14, 16, 18, 20, 23, 24, 26 (notebook) BeatWalk/Shutterstock.com; p. 4 (desert)
Doug Lemke/Shutterstock.com; p. 4 (cactus) Roberto Chicano/Shutterstock.com; p. 5 dmodlin01/Shutterstock.com;
p. 6 (inset) Angel DiBilio/Shutterstock.com; p. 6 (main) Aspen Photo/Shutterstock.com; p. 6 (raindrops)
Ramaniy Volha/Shutterstock.com; p. 7 OFFFSTOCK/Shutterstock.com; p. 8 Daniel Novak/Moment/Getty Images;
p. 9 (fire), 16 (doodle) advent/Shutterstock.com; p. 9 Travel Ink/Gallo Images/Getty Images; p. 10 Don Emmert/
AFP/Getty Images; pp. 10–11 Jonas Gratzer/Light Rocket/Getty Images; pp. 12–13 Daniel Kreher/Getty Images;
p. 14 (bottom inset) Nature Art/Shutterstock.com; p. 14 (middle inset) Pavel Tvrdy/Shutterstock.com; p. 14 (top
inset) Shane Myers Photography/Shutterstock.com; p. 14 (main) iofoto/Shutterstock.com; p. 15 Carini Joe/
Perspectives/Getty Images; p. 16 Wendy Shattil and Bob Rozinski/Oxford Scientific/Getty Images; pp. 17 (map),
18 (map), 21 (map) Rainier Lesniewski/Shutterstock.com; p. 18 (mountains) Emre Tarimcioglu/Shutterstock.com;
p. 19 Arsgera/Shutterstock.com; p. 20 Josemaria Toscano/Shutterstock.com; p. 21 (main) Pete McBride/
National Geographic Magazines/Getty Images; p. 22 (left) S-F/Shutterstock.com; p. 22 (right) Fort Worth
Star-Telegram/Tribune News Service/Getty Images; p. 23 Zack Frank/Shutterstock.com; p. 24 (inset) Aleksey
Stemmer/Shutterstock.com; pp. 24–25 (main) Nate Biletnikoff/Antarctic Photo Library/National Science
Foundation; pp. 25 (inset), 29 (bottom inset) Peter Rejcek/Antarctic Photo Library/National Science Foundation;
p. 26 (inset) Rob Jones/Getty Images Europe/Getty Images; pp. 26–27 (main) Anton_Ivanov/Shutterstock.com;
p. 27 (inset) Nicolle Rager-Fuller/NSF/Wikimedia Commons; pp. 28–29 (map) VanHart/Shutterstock.com; p. 28
(top inset) Wollertz/Shutterstock.com; p. 28 (bottom inset) courtesy of NASA; p. 29 (top inset) Brocken Inaglory/
Wikimedia Commons; p. 29 (middle inset) Auscape/Universal Images Group/Getty Images.

Printed in the United States of America

CPSIA compliance information: Batch #CS16GS: For further information contact Gareth Stevens, New York, New York at 1-800-542-2595.

Contents

The Graben of Death 4

Lands of Fire 8

Hell on Earth 12

Fire Islands 14

All Your Fault! 16

Making Mountains 18

The Grand Wait 20

Say What? 22

All About Antarctica 24

The Map of Weird Geography 28

Glossary 30

For More Information 31

Index 32

Words in the glossary appear in **bold** type the first time they are used in the text.

THE GRABEN OF DEATH

If you're not careful, you can die in Death Valley. The basin, located in California, is one of the hottest places on Earth. With its lowest point at 282 feet (86 m) below sea level, it also holds the lowest point in North America. The valley is a graben, or a broken part of Earth's crust that has sunk into the ground.

Q: How did Death Valley get its name?

A: Some very angry travelers gave this **geographic** area its name. In 1849, people headed to the California gold fields got lost in the large basin for 2 months. When they finally found their way out, one traveler said, "Good-bye, Death Valley." The name stuck.

Despite the dangers in Death Valley, about a million people visit Death Valley National Park each year!

HOT Air

On July 10, 1913, the air at Furnace Creek measured 134°F (57°C)! That's the hottest air temperature ever recorded on Earth. Summertime in Death Valley can mean temperatures around 120°F (49°C), even in the shade! Don't worry. Temperatures might finally drop to double digits at night.

Death Valley has lots of different geographical features to explore. The basin is surrounded by mountain peaks tipped with snow that feature plenty of hiking trails. It's also far from dead: more than 1,000 different plants and plenty of animals call Death Valley home. There are even some fish!

Q: Does it ever rain in Death Valley?

A: Sometimes! Rainfall averages less than 2 inches (5 cm) a year, which is much less than most deserts. Late-summer thunderstorms, however, can cause flooding! It's mostly sunny in Death Valley, but winter storms or summer rains can bring cloud cover. And when it rains, wildflowers grow in the valley!

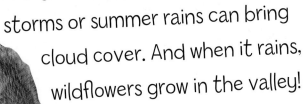

coyotes

TELESCOPE PEAK

The driest recorded period in Death Valley is a 40-month stretch from 1931 to 1934 when only 0.64 inch (1.6 cm) of rain fell. No rain was recorded in 1929 or 1953!

A Grand DROP

The highest peak in Death Valley National Park–Telescope Peak–is 11,049 feet (3,368 m) tall. Just 15 miles (24 km) away is Badwater Basin, the lowest point in the United States. The drop between the two is twice as deep as the Grand Canyon!

LANDS OF FIRE

There are two kinds of geography: physical and human. Physical geography studies the natural features of landforms and how they came about, while human geography studies how human activity affects Earth's **environments**. Fire, which can be caused naturally or by people, has greatly affected Earth geographically in many ways.

The Eternal FLAME

A natural gas pocket in Chestnut Ridge County Park in New York State allows a flame to flicker while surrounded by water. Called Eternal Flame Falls, the gas is produced naturally and may have been first lit by Native Americans long ago. The flame, however, *does* go out sometimes. Hikers use lighters to keep it burning!

Q: How long can a fire burn on Earth?

A: If there's a source of fuel and oxygen, a fire can burn forever! In Australia, a **coal seam** fire underneath Mount Wingen has burned for more than 5,000 years. People think a lightning strike may have hit the seam, starting the fire.

MOUNT WINGEN

In the 1800s, explorers who came across Mount Wingen—or Burning Mountain—thought the smoking peak was a **volcano**! The fire won't go out until it runs out of coal to burn.

Mine Fires

Not all long-term fires start naturally. When mines are dug to search for coal and other **natural resources**, fires that burn for years can be sparked. China, the United States, and many other countries are dealing with mine fires burning right now!

A fire in a coal mine beneath the town of Centralia, Pennsylvania, has burned since 1962. Scientists expect it to burn for another 250 years as it runs through about 8 miles (13 km) of coal.

COAL SEAM FIRE UNDER CENTRALIA, PENNSYLVANIA

Dangerous Living

Coal seam fires are dangerous to those living nearby. Fires can give off sulfur and other gases that poison the air and water supply. The never-ending fires can even make the ground near the heat of the flames unstable—and cause **collapse**!

Striking Fire

A fire set by miners on strike in New Straitsville, Ohio, has burned underground since 1884. The government had to help contain the fire before it destroyed the rest of the town. It's expected to burn for another century! The New Straitsville History Group said people living in town fried eggs over fire holes!

COAL MINE FIRE IN INDIA

HeLL on EARTH

Q: What the heck made the Door to Hell?

A: Humans did! The central Asian country of Turkmenistan has the world's sixth-largest supply of natural gas buried underground. No one knows for sure how the Door to Hell—or Darvaza Crater—was created, as there's no known official record of activity there. But a common story goes like this: In 1971, a **Soviet** group drilled into the ground and hit a big pocket of natural gas. The ground gave way, creating a large crater 225 feet (69 m) wide and 99 feet (30 m) deep. Scientists decided to set a fire, thinking it would stop a dangerous release of natural gas into the air. But supplied by the natural gas reserve below, the fire hasn't stopped burning for **decades**!

Diving In

In 2013, explorer George Kourounis actually went into the Darvaza Crater! He took samples and measured the hole wearing special gear so he didn't get burned.

FIRE ISLANDS

Q: Is Hawaii getting bigger?

A: Yes, but very slowly. The Big Island of Hawaii adds more than 42 acres (17 ha) per year because of the Kīlauea volcano, which has erupted continuously for 30 years! One of the largest volcanoes in the world, Mauna Loa, is also on the island.

Strange Sands

Beaches in Hawaii can be yellow, black, green, and even red! The volcanic activity on the island means many different rocks, shells, and minerals break down over time to create different sand colors.

Magma to Lava TO ROCK

Volcanoes occur when melted rock called magma is forced out through Earth's crust. When the magma reaches the surface, it's called lava. When lava cools, it forms rock. Anytime lava is flowing from a volcano, it's called an eruption. Sometimes lava **oozes** out slowly. Other times, huge amounts of lava, rock, and gases are forced violently out of a volcanic hot spot.

ALL YOUR FAULT!

The San Andreas Fault is one of the most **distinctive** landmarks in California. It formed about 28 million years ago when two large **tectonic plates** ran into each other. When these plates move, it causes **earthquakes**!

Q: Is the San Andreas the only fault in California?

A: No, but it's the biggest and most easily seen. California has the most faults of any US state. Other major faults, such as the Hayward Fault, run **parallel** to the San Andreas Fault. The San Andreas Fault caused major earthquakes in Fort Tejon in 1857 and in San Francisco in 1906.

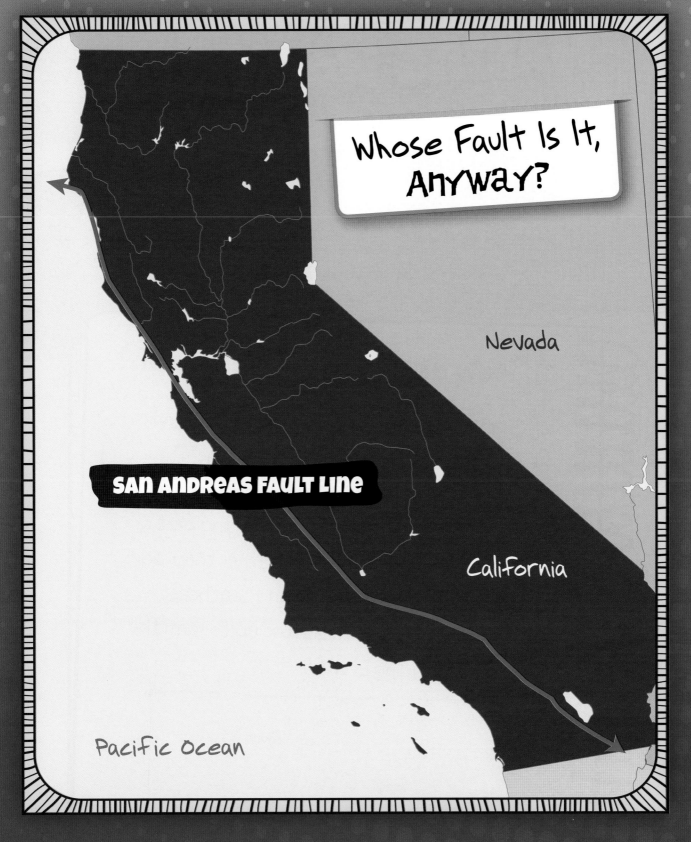

Whose Fault Is It, Anyway?

SAN ANDREAS FAULT LINE

Nevada

California

Pacific Ocean

A fault is a place within Earth where rock is broken, often at the edge of where tectonic plates meet. Plates can slide past one another, move in opposite directions, or even crash into one another. A fault line is where a fault shows on Earth's surface. Faults and fault lines are commonly the sites of **seismic** activity. There are faults all over the United States. Most are buried underground.

MAKING MOUNTAINS

Mount Everest in Nepal is the highest peak on Earth. It rises more than 29,000 feet (8,840 m) above sea level. Only a few thousand people have ever braved the cold, thin air, and height of Everest to reach its **summit**.

Q: How did Mount Everest form?

A: Mount Everest grew up when two tectonic plates collided over a long period of time. The continental plate of modern-day India plowed northward into Asia and Europe, causing part of Earth's crust to shoot upward. Rather than slide under the Indian plate, China and Southeast Asia resisted and eventually rose up to form the Himalayas, including Everest.

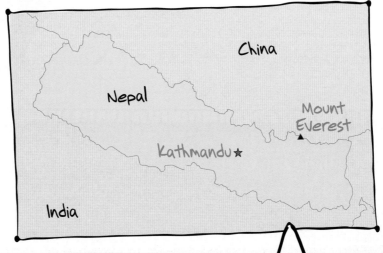

Most **geologists** call any landform that rises at least 1,000 feet (305 m) or more above the area surrounding it a mountain.

Moving MOUNTAINS

In 2015, a deadly earthquake hit Nepal. The quake was so powerful it actually made Mount Everest a bit shorter. An area of ground measuring 75 miles (121 km) long and 30 miles (48 km) wide near the city of Kathmandu lifted up about 3 feet (0.9 m).

Water and wind can be powerful forces in the shaping of Earth's physical geography, but one key ingredient in the creation of landforms is time. Mount Everest took millions of years to form, but give wind and water that kind of time, and they, too, will make some amazing things.

Q: What created the Grand Canyon?

A: Scientists believe a combination of a few different things did. The massive **gorge** is 277 miles (446 km) long, 18 miles (29 km) wide at one point, and about 6,000 feet (1,829 m) deep. Much of it was formed by the flow of the Colorado River, which sits at the bottom of the canyon. Its flow **eroded** the rock over a long, long time.

Q: What about that wind?

A: It certainly played its part, too. Wind forcing sand and other **debris** against the canyon walls uncovered about 40 different rock layers, which gives the Grand Canyon its different colors.

The Colorado River touches five states, but the Grand Canyon sits entirely inside the state of Arizona.

NV

UT

Colorado River →

CO

CA

← Grand Canyon

AZ

NM

Pacific Ocean

SAY WHAT?

Learning about geography can be confusing because there are lots of different places that have the same name. The country of Georgia, for example, is very different from the US state! Lots of cities share a name, too. In the United States alone, there are more than 20 cities named after Paris, France. Many of them, like Paris, Texas, built their own **version** of France's Eiffel Tower!

PARIS, TEXAS

PARIS, FRANCE

Q: Why is Arkansas not pronounced like Kansas?

A: The easy answer is the difference between the French and English languages. Both states were named after Native American groups. English-speaking settlers named Kansas after the Kansa. Arkansas was named after the Algonquian word for the Quapaw. It was spelled different ways, though, and the French version—Arcansas—was what eventually won out.

Say It Right... IT'S The Law

In 1881, there was an argument between two Arkansas state senators about how to say the state's name. The state **legislature** had to make an official ruling that "AR-kan-saw" is the correct pronunciation.

ALL ABOUT ANTARCTICA

Of the seven continents, the one with the lowest population is Antarctica. This is because it's the coldest place on Earth! Only scientists doing research have ever called the continent home. There's never been an **indigenous** human population on Antarctica, which means it's the only continent on Earth to ever truly be discovered by explorers!

Q: Is Antarctica really a desert?

A: Yes! Not only is it the coldest place on Earth, the fifth-largest continent is also geographically considered a desert. Antarctica gets about 0.2 inch (5 mm) of **precipitation** a year near the South Pole. It's so cold there, the snow that does fall never melts, which builds up glaciers over a long period of time.

The closest thing to a city on Antarctica is McMurdo Station, which first opened in 1956. It's home to scientists studying Antarctica and the wildlife living there.

Q: Does a country own Antarctica?

A: Seven different countries have claimed territory in Antarctica—Argentina, Australia, Chile, France, New Zealand, Norway, and the United Kingdom. In 1959, nations with scientists working on Antarctica signed the Antarctic Treaty, which says the continent will be used for "peaceful purposes only." Today, 53 different nations have signed the treaty, including the United States and Russia, who both have a "basis of claim" to Antarctica.

IT'S Alive!

In 2012, Russian scientists drilled through more than 2 miles (3.2 km) of ice into Lake Vostok, a large ancient lake under a glacier. Scientists found lots of different DNA in the water samples taken from the lake. They think the lake may contain thousands of different tiny organisms and even fish!

Drill

Glacier

Lake Vostok

ANTARCTICA

South Pole

Lake Vostok

The coldest temperature ever recorded in Antarctica is −129.3°F (−89.6°C)! But only the top of Lake Vostok freezes because under 2 miles (3.2 km) of ice it's closer to Earth's warm core.

The Map of
WEiRD GEOGRAPHY

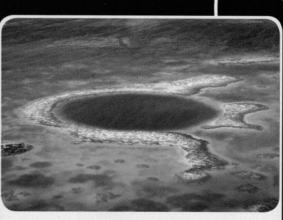

Great Blue Hole,
Lighthouse Reef, Belize

Off the coast of Belize, Great Blue Hole
is the largest sinkhole on Earth!

Eye of the Sahara, Mauritania

The Richat Structure looks like a bull's-eye
in the middle of the desert.

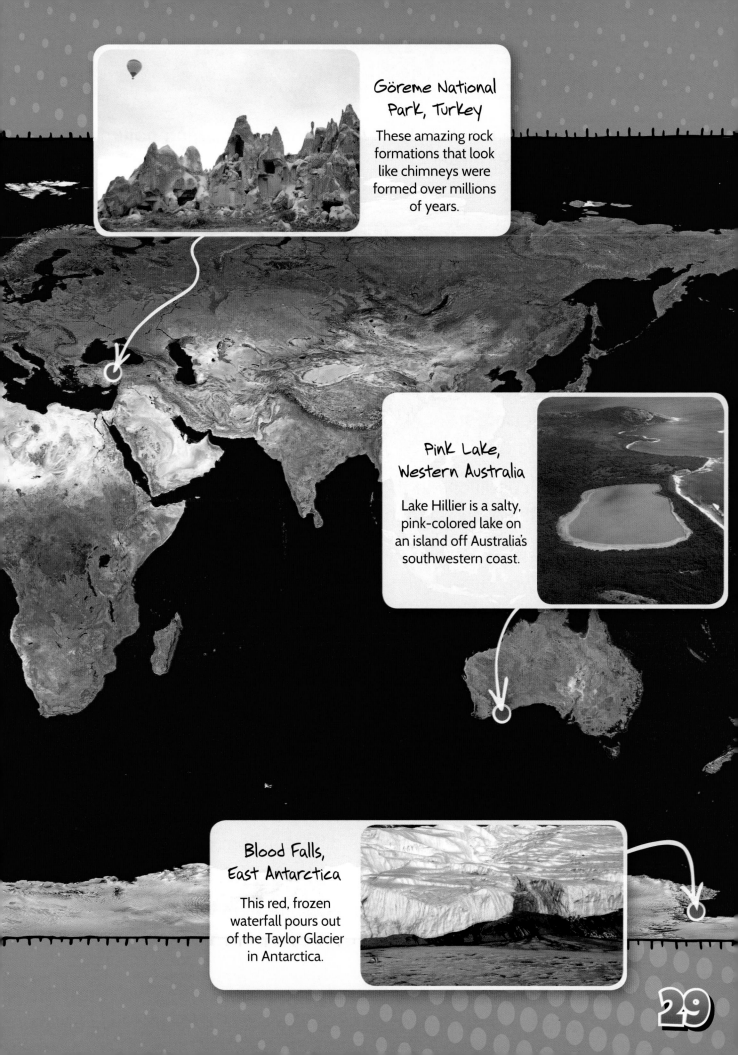

Göreme National Park, Turkey

These amazing rock formations that look like chimneys were formed over millions of years.

Pink Lake, Western Australia

Lake Hillier is a salty, pink-colored lake on an island off Australia's southwestern coast.

Blood Falls, East Antarctica

This red, frozen waterfall pours out of the Taylor Glacier in Antarctica.

Glossary

coal seam: a large deposit of coal found in a certain area

collapse: to cave in

debris: the remains of something that has been broken

decade: a period of 10 years

distinctive: having to do with being set apart from others

earthquake: a shaking or trembling of Earth's crust

environment: the conditions that surround a living thing and affect the way it lives

erode: to wear away outer layers of rock or soil by the action of wind and water

geographic: having to do with the science of areas where living and nonliving things exist on Earth and how they affect one another

geologist: someone who studies the history of Earth, especially its formations and rocks

gorge: a narrow, steep-walled canyon or part of a canyon

indigenous: occurring naturally in a place

legislature: a lawmaking body

natural resource: something found in nature that people can use

ooze: to flow or leak slowly

parallel: laying in the same direction as another thing

precipitation: rain, snow, sleet, or hail

seismic: having to do with an earthquake

Soviet: having to do with the Union of Soviet Socialist Republics, much of which is modern Russia

summit: the top of a mountain

tectonic plate: one of the movable pieces of rock that create Earth's surface

version: a form of something that is different from others

volcano: an opening in a planet's surface through which hot, liquid rock sometimes flows

BOOKS

Gilbert, Sara. *Death Valley.* Mankato, MN: Creative Education, 2016.

Hawkins, John. *The World's Strangest Unexplained Mysteries.* New York, NY: PowerKids Press, 2012.

Marsico, Katie. *The Highest and the Lowest.* New York, NY: Children's Press, 2016.

WEBSITES

McMurdo Station Webcams
usap.gov/videoclipsandmaps/mcmwebcam.cfm
Check out a live view of one of the few inhabited places on Antarctica.

The San Andreas Fault
geology.com/articles/san-andreas-fault.shtml
Learn more about California's San Andreas Fault here.

Volcano Facts
ngkids.co.uk/science-and-nature/Volcano-Facts
Find out many fun facts and watch a video all about volcanoes!

Publisher's note to educators and parents: Our editors have carefully reviewed these websites to ensure that they are suitable for students. Many websites change frequently, however, and we cannot guarantee that a site's future contents will continue to meet our high standards of quality and educational value. Be advised that students should be closely supervised whenever they access the Internet.

#

Antarctica 24, 25, 26, 27, 29

Badwater Basin 7

Blood Falls 29

Centralia, Pennsylvania 10

coal seam fire 9, 11

Darvaza Crater 12, 13

Death Valley 4, 5, 6, 7

Door to Hell 12

earthquakes 16, 19

Eye of the Sahara 28

Eternal Flame Falls 8

Furnace Creek 5

Göreme National Park 29

graben 4

Grand Canyon 7, 20, 21

Great Blue Hole 28

Hayward Fault 16

Kīlauea 14

Lake Vostok 27

Mauna Loa 14

Mount Everest 18, 19, 20

Mount Wingen 9

New Straitsville, Ohio 11

Pink Lake 29

San Andreas Fault 16

tectonic plates 16, 17, 18

Telescope Peak 7